VILLA-LOBOS

A PROLE DO BEBÊ NO. 1 FOR THE PIANO
(The Baby's Family)

EDITED BY DAVID P. APPLEBY

AN ALFRED MASTERWORK EDITION

Alfred Music Publishing Co., Inc.
P.O. Box 10003
Van Nuys, CA 91410-0003
alfred.com

Book Alone:
ISBN-10: 0-7390-8036-9
ISBN-13: 978-0-7390-8036-8

Book & CD:
ISBN-10: 0-7390-7758-9
ISBN-13: 978-0-7390-7758-0

Cover art: The Child with the Doll
by Henri Rousseau
Musée de l'Orangerie, Paris, France
Scala Fine Arts/Art Resource, New York

HEITOR VILLA-LOBOS
A prole do bebê no. 1
(The Baby's Family)

Edited by David P. Appleby

CONTENTS

A rare photo of
Lucilia Guimarães Villa-Lobos,
the composer's wife, to whom
A prole do bebê no. 1 *is dedicated.*

Introduction

On Wednesday, November 22, 1944, while the United States was at war with Germany and Japan, a 57-year-old Brazilian composer, Heitor Villa-Lobos, arrived at the Los Angeles airport. Because he was scheduled to receive an honorary doctorate from Occidental College that evening and his plane was late, he arrived at the auditorium of the college under police escort, with sirens going full blast, just minutes before the commencement service began. This dramatic debut of Villa-Lobos in the United States seems appropriate to a composer who was soon heralded by U.S. critics as a "sensation" and the "czar of Latin American music." It was rumored that he had written several thousand musical works. In a relatively short time, his music became identified with his native country, Brazil, like that of no composer before or since. His music reflects the full range of the rhythmic richness and diversity of the urban music of his Afro-Brazilian heritage.

Although in 1944 Villa-Lobos was known to a limited number of American musicians, his fame in Europe was well established. His best-known piano work was a suite of pieces dedicated to his wife, Lucilia Guimarães Villa-Lobos (1886–1966), *A prole do bebê no 1*. The work was first performed in Rio de Janeiro, Brazil, on July 5, 1922, by the pianist Arthur Rubinstein. Rubinstein was an admirer of Villa-Lobos and had a significant impact on his career, both as a performer of his music and as a friend who introduced him to wealthy patrons. An introduction by Rubinstein to a wealthy Brazilian, Carlos Guinle, resulted in a sponsorship that made it possible for Villa-Lobos to make his first two trips to Europe and to perform and publish his music there. In his introduction, Rubinstein said to Guinle, "Right here in Brazil lives an authentic genius, in my opinion the only one on the whole American continent. His country does not understand him, but future generations will be proud of him."[1]

[1]Arthur Rubinstein, *My Many Years* (New York: Alfred A. Knopf, 1980), 155.

PROGRAMMA

Quarta-feira, 5 de Julho de 1922

3.º concerto do famoso pianista

Arthur RUBINSTEIN

Tocata e Fuga...............................	**BACH - TAUSIG**
Preludio, Coral e Fuga......................	**CESAR FRANCK**

A Prole do Bébé.............................		**H. VILLA LOBOS**
Branquinha..........	a boneca de louça	
Moreninha..........	massa	
Caboclinha	barro	
A Pobresinha........	trapo	
Negrinha	páo	
Bruxa	panno	
O Polichinello		

Barcarola, Op. 60	}	**CHOPIN**
Dois estudos..........................	}	
Rêve d'amour	}	**LISZT**
Rhapsodia XII........................	}	

Grande piano de concerto — Bösendorfer — cedido pela Escola de Musica Figueiredo Roxo

About This Edition

A prole do bebê no. 1 was written in 1918 and was first published that same year by Arthur Napoleão, one of Brazil's oldest publishing firms, and distributed by Gustavo Sampaio, the firm possessing distribution rights at the time. The work was later published in Paris by Max Eschig. After the first Brazilian and French editions, numerous other editions were published in Brazil, France and the United States. Various editions of "O polichinelo," the most popular movement of the suite, were also published separately.

With a number of editions of this work already in print, why is a new edition needed? The most important reason is that a complete performing edition of this popular set of pieces is essential in light of the interest in the music of Villa-Lobos resulting from performances during the Villa-Lobos Centennial celebrations in 1987–88. The Napoleão and Eschig editions contain only a few pedalings and no fingerings. The access of the editor to a 1918 Napoleão edition furnished by the Museu Villa-Lobos in Rio de Janeiro with markings in the hand of the composer and extensive new research into the music of Villa-Lobos provide new insights into the performance of his music.

David P. Appleby, the editor of this edition, was one of four Americans honored by the Brazilian government in 1988 with the Villa-Lobos Centennial Medal, for his outstanding research into the life and music of Heitor Villa-Lobos. Dr. Appleby was born in Brazil 300 miles from the birthplace of Villa-Lobos, and has made the study of his music a lifelong pursuit.

The aim of this edition is to provide the pianist with an authentic text based on the 1918 Napoleão edition and performance traditions that have become a part of this work. The editor has provided pedal markings and fingerings (along with other editorial markings that appear in parentheses), but has not sought to change the original score, which contains expression and tempo markings in Portuguese, French and Italian. The use of these three languages has been retained in this edition. English translations have been provided where they seemed appropriate or necessary.

Style

Arthur Rubinstein's premier performance of *A prole do bebê no. 1* consisted of seven of the eight movements ("Mulatinha," the fourth movement, was omitted). Rubinstein reversed the order of the last two movements and concluded with "O polichinelo." Many recordings follow Rubinstein's example, inverting the order of the last two movements and playing "O polichinelo" as the final movement.

In his biography, Rubinstein relates a colorful, although somewhat inaccurate, account of a lunch with Villa-Lobos at which the composer told him about a set of pieces he had written for his wife, Lucilia. According to Rubinstein, Villa-Lobos sent him the music the next day. Rubinstein was quite amused at Villa-Lobos's exaggerated manner of speech and quotes him as saying that he had traveled throughout Brazil gathering folkloric material and that he had discovered the "secret soul" of his country.[2]

In the 1918 Napoleão edition of *A prole do bebê no. 1*, titles and markings are in Portuguese, while many of the expression and tempo markings are in French and Italian, with no apparent effort at consistency. Because references are made in various sources to the movements in all three languages, the editor has provided titles and subtitles of the movements as they appear in various editions.

Portuguese (Napoleão edition)	French (Eschig edition)	English (Edward B. Marks edition)
1. BRANQUINHA A boneca de louça	Petite blanche La poupée de biscuit	The Little White Doll The Porcelain Doll
2. MORENINHA A boneca de massa	Petite brune La poupée de papier maché	The Little Brunette Doll The Papier-Mâché Doll
3. CABOCLINHA A boneca de barro	Petite indigène du Brésil La poupée de argile	The Little Copper-Colored Doll The Clay Doll
4. MULATINHA A boneca de borracha	Petite mulatresse La poupée de caoutchoue	The Little Mulatto Doll The Rubber Doll
5. NEGRINHA A boneca de pau	Petite negresse La poupée en bois	The Little Black Doll The Wooden Doll
6. A POBREZINHA A boneca de trapo	Petite pauvre La poupée de chiffons	The Poor Little Doll The Rag Doll
7. O POLICHINELO (Villa Lobos used no subtitle)	Le polichinel	The Punch Doll
8. BRUXA A boneca de pano	Sorcière La poupée de drap	The Witch Doll The Cloth Doll

[2]Ibid., 92.

Brazil is a multiracial society with a rich ethnic diversity. It is not unusual to find Brazilian families in which the skin color of family members ranges from near white to almost completely black. The doll family depicted in this collection represents the ethnic diversity of such a family, and the baby enjoys all of the dolls. According to Dona Maria Augusta Machado, Museologist at the Museu Villa-Lobos (the principal repository of the Villa Lobos's manuscripts), it is important to remember that ethnic differences imply social differences, and the child plays with her dolls during the period of her life when maternal consciousness and awareness of social differences are beginning to develop.

The titles of the first six movements of *A prole do bebê no. 1* indicate the ethnic or folk character of each doll in the baby's collection. The subtitles indicate the type of doll (porcelain, papier-mâché, clay, rag, rubber, etc.).

At the time Villa-Lobos wrote this work, white porcelain dolls (portrayed in the first movement) were usually quite expensive, since they were imported from France and had human hair. This was a doll to be admired, not loved, and to be handled with great care. The brunette doll is much more typically Brazilian, her dark skin showing the generations of intermarriage typical of middle-class families. She is very cuddly and loves to play. The *Caboclinha*, a doll of copper-colored hue, represents babies of mixed Indian and Portuguese descent and is made of pottery, an art in which the Indian population excels. Experienced hands have crafted her beauty, and the child enjoys playing with her. *Mulatinha*, the mulatto doll, made of rubber, is a reminder of the largest segment of society and is soft to the touch. *Negrinha*, the black doll, made of cloth, represents the poorest children that are a part of the ethnic family. She and *Pobrezinha*, the poor doll, must be loved and held. The dolls complete the baby's family, and are often kept throughout childhood and into adolescence, awakening happy memories of early childhood.[3] As a child's imagination clothes each doll with its own individual personality, the differences of character of each doll must be part of a sensitive performance of *A prole do bebê no. 1.*

[3]Dona Maria Augusta Machado, "Villa-Lobos e sua prole," unpublished essay, no date.

A' Lucilia Villa-Lobos

A Próle do Bébé (Nº 1)
(LA FAMILLE DU BÉBÉ)
COLLECÇÃO DE PEÇAS CARACTERISTICAS

1 BRANQUINHA – A boneca de louça.
(Petite blanche – La poupée de biscuit)

Rio, *1918.*

H. VILLA-LOBOS

8006

Villa-Lobos and Folk Music

Like many of Villa-Lobos's works, *A prole do bebê no. 1* makes extensive use of music familiar to Brazilians of his day. Some of the melodies Villa-Lobos incorporated are still popular and can be easily recognized by many Brazilians. Unfortunately, a generation of children and young adults in both the United States and Brazil has grown up with little knowledge of the folk tunes of its ancestors. In this volume, when a Brazilian melody is quoted in fairly complete form several times, such as "Dorme, nenê" (Sleep, Baby) in "Branquinha," the melody is identified in a footnote. When only a portion of the melody appears, or when the melody is not familiar to the editor, no indication appears. It is nevertheless important to realize that Villa-Lobos borrowed abundantly from the melodies of his day.

Interviews with Villa-Lobos frequently touched on his compositions' relationship to Brazilian folk music. In one interview, Villa-Lobos was asked about the source of his melodies. He replied, "Eu sou folclore" ("I am folklore, and the melodies I compose are as truly folk music as those I have collected"). On another occasion Villa-Lobos was closely questioned by a reporter in New York about his use of ancient Indian melodies, which were virtually unknown to Indians of the present day. The reporter asked, "Maestro, if the melodies are unknown at the present time, how did you obtain them?" Villa-Lobos, who loved a practical joke, replied, "From parrots. In Brazil, parrots have great longevity. There are parrots who heard the melodies many years ago. They learned them, and when I traveled through the jungles of Brazil, the parrots sang the folk tunes to me."[4] Since Villa-Lobos spoke little English, such multilingual exchanges made him an even greater sensation than the concerts of his music.

The most frequent source of melodies in Villa-Lobos's works is the *Guia prático*, a practical guide to Brazilian folk music compiled by the composer. Published in the 1930s, this six-volume set contains music collected over several decades. According to Villa-Lobos's own commentary on the collection, many of these melodies were sung in public schools and were of European origin.

---

[4]This story was related to the editor by Brazilian composer Edino Krieger, who was present at the interview in the late 1940s.

Heitor Villa-Lobos

Pedaling

Perhaps the most difficult part of the editor's work has been the addition of pedal markings. Villa-Lobos frequently called for long pedalings with no pedal changes for various harmonic changes and was insistent that these pedalings be observed. Some passages call for absolute clarity of sound, others for blurred combinations of chordal sounds.

In this edition, the traditional style pedal symbol (℗.) and pedal release (✱) are used to display Villa-Lobos's pedal indications, while the modern style pedal notation (└────∧────┘) is used to display the editor's pedal indications. When both the composer's and editor's pedalings are present, the editor's indications appear beneath those of the composer.

In "Branquinha," Villa-Lobos calls for pedal on page 16 and a pedal release appears on page 19. It is unlikely but not impossible that the composer meant for this entire section, in which the melody appears primarily in a register of the piano in which the keys lack dampers, to be played with the damper pedal depressed throughout. In measure 14 of "Branquinha," Villa-Lobos provides a pedal marking (℗.) but does not indicate where the pedal should be released. It appears that the composer sometimes would indicate with the word ℗. that the damper pedal should be used in a given section without noting the exact manner or duration of the pedaling. In such circumstances, the editor has provided a suggested pedaling. In measures 47–49 of the same piece, there are several changes of harmony per measure, and Villa-Lobos insists that a single pedaling be used throughout the three measures. He even adds the word *sempre* to emphasize his insistence on the single unchanged pedaling. If the student of this edition finds some long pedalings unacceptable, pedal changes may be made more frequently, but the editor has sought to maintain pedaling consistent with the performance traditions of this work and the known intent of the composer.

Pedaling must always be conceived at a performance tempo. Under no circumstances should the composer's or editor's pedaling be used when practicing the piece slowly. Since pedaling represents a segment of time, to employ the composer or editor's pedaling while practicing a piece at half the performance tempo means in actuality that twice as much pedal is being used.

About the Music

The opening mood of the aristocratic doll piece is set in a four-measure phrase beginning with quarter-note chords. The entire phrase is to be played in a single pedal, which appears in the original Napoleão edition. The stately beginning builds in intensity with 16th notes, an *affretando* (hurrying) in measure 11, a glissando in measure 13, and the first complete folk tune quotation in measure 16. Usually Villa-Lobos avoids complete melody quotations, but the lullaby "Dorme, nenê" (Sleep, Baby) appears several times in the piece. The first time, the notes of the melody are to be played detached; Villa-Lobos adds the instruction "as sung by a small child." In measure 60 the melody occurs again, two octaves higher. The entire section is marked with a pedal indication in measure 57 and a release in measure 89—32 1/2 measures later! The changing harmonies and the low bass tones produce an ethereal mood for the performer daring enough to use Villa-Lobos's original pedaling. In this section the lullaby theme ("Dorme, nenê") appears in augmentation in the right hand. Since the upper keys of the piano have no dampers, the chord changes must be played softly if the gentle blurring is to be effective.

A papier-mâché doll is not a thing of beauty. Easily obtainable in any of Rio's numerous small shops, papier-mâché dolls are relatively inexpensive and are made of the same material used for masks and many other Carnival decorations. The jovial mood of the piece indicates the carefree attitude of a child playing with the doll that can be handled and cuddled without the apprehension needed toward the porcelain doll, which would be expensive to replace and is not a play doll. Papier-mâché dolls are often ugly, some actually grotesque, since their makers are not concerned with making a work of art. Children have fun playing with them, and the bouncing mood of this piece describes the joy of a child playing with a brunette doll.

Caboclinha 25
The word *caboclo* has many different meanings in Portuguese, the most common being "copper colored," or person of Indian and Portuguese descent. The feminine diminutive form, *caboclinha*, is used here for a small, copper-colored clay doll. The musical setting is in duple meter, the most common meter for Brazilian urban music, and the rhythmic pattern within the duple setting is 3+3+2, one of the most typically Brazilian rhythms. Villa-Lobos instructs the player to smoothly connect the pattern. In the third measure, the introduction of a triplet in the left hand against the syncopation in the right hand produces a sensuously undulating feeling common to the Brazilian samba. This feeling is reinforced in measure 7 by a melody beginning with a tied-over second beat. The syncopation here creates a mood of languorous (*moureusement*), slow and caressing sensuality. The child may understand little about sensuality, but the rhythms and the music are a part of everyday childhood experiences.

Mulatinha 30
A kaleidoscopic series of tempo and texture changes and the alternation of metrical sections and cadenzalike figurations convey the idea of playfulness, fun and childhood freedom. Mischievous unpedaled staccato sections and a folk melody complete this little gem, posing a challenge for the player with a lively imagination. The folk melody, introduced in measure 12, is "Vem cá, Bitú," a melody that has persisted in Brazilian folk song literature in various forms. The melody is also used with a text sung on St. John's Day, "Cai, cai, balão" (Fall, Fall, Balloon). St. John's Day is a religious festival observed on June 24 every year. A major event of the festivities is the release of hot air balloons, which fill the sky as observers dance and sing the song "Cai, cai, balão." The repeated references to this song in "Mulatinha" depict a child's recollection of happy memories of St. John's Day.

Negrinha 36
The black doll is represented by a joyous and lively movement in 16th notes. In "Negrinha" Villa-Lobos quotes the opening melody of the folk song "Uma, duas angolinhas," which appears as No. 124 in the *Guia prático*. The *angolinha* is a guinea hen, a pheasantlike bird thought to be from Africa but commonly found in Brazil.

A pobrezinha 42
In this movement, the shortest of the eight, Villa-Lobos shows himself a master of creating moods with a minimum of musical materials. Here the universal popularity of rag dolls among children and the earliest awakening of maternal feelings are portrayed musically with a slow tempo and an ascending, melancholy, five-note minor figure in a minor key after a two-measure introduction. Rather than quote a folk theme exactly, Villa-Lobos introduces a melody that duplicates the intervalic outline of "A canoa virou," No. 23 in the *Guia prático*.[5] The melody in the *Guia prático* is a song about an overturned boat. One interesting feature of this melody is the constant shift from major to minor mode. "A pobrezinha" is a small gem that contrasts sharply with the joyous mood of "Negrinha," the movement that precedes it, and the ever-popular "O polichinelo," which follows.

[5]David P. Appleby, *The Music of Brazil* (Austin, Texas: University of Texas Press, 1983), 126.

This movement is unquestionably the single-most popular piano piece written by Villa-Lobos. Often performed separately and usually played as the closing movement of *A prole do bebê no. 1*, this movement contains a quotation of "Ciranda, cirandinha," a well-known Brazilian folk tune. The extremely rapid tempo at which "O polichinelo" is usually performed creates a mood of joyous buffoonery and depicts the enjoyment of a child remembering the chief character in a puppet show.

Brazil's African heritage is steeped in spirits, and Brazilian religious culture has combined elements of animistic religions and Roman Catholicism in a unique and colorful way. Bruxa reminds the child of this world of evil spirits, in which witches and evil spirits abound. While this world is frightening, protection is usually nearby in the arms of a mother or African nursemaid who understands witches and evil spirits. Witches have long been a favorite subject of composers, and Villa-Lobos's portrayal evokes visions of sudden, mysterious appearances; unexplained disappearances; and whimsical changes of mood through changes of dynamics and tempo. In this movement Villa-Lobos shows himself a master of imagination and the world of evil spirits. Strange chromaticisms, polychordal textures, rapid chains of augmented chords, and a rich palette of unusual harmonic effects create an atmosphere of the mysterious world inhabited by witches and evil spirits.

Acknowledgments

I am grateful to the following individuals and institutions for their invaluable assistance in the preparation of this edition: Martha Appleby, for help in every phase of editing; Dr. Don Krummel, Professor of Bibliography at the University of Illinois; Ann Hartness, Librarian, Nettie Lee Benson Latin American Collection of the University of Texas; Fran Balsam, Cataloging Unit Manager, Fort Worth Public Library; the Museu Villa-Lobos, Rio de Janeiro, for providing access to the earliest Arthur Napoleão edition with markings by the composer; and most especially Dona Maria Augusta Machado, Museologist, for her valuable comments on the Brazilian dolls depicted in this work.

To Lucilia Villa-Lobos

BRANQUINHA
A BONECA DE LOUÇA ⓐ

Heitor Villa-Lobos
(1887–1959)

ⓐ Title and translation: *Branquinha* (The Little White Doll)
Subtitle and translation: *A boneca de louça* (The Porcelain Doll)

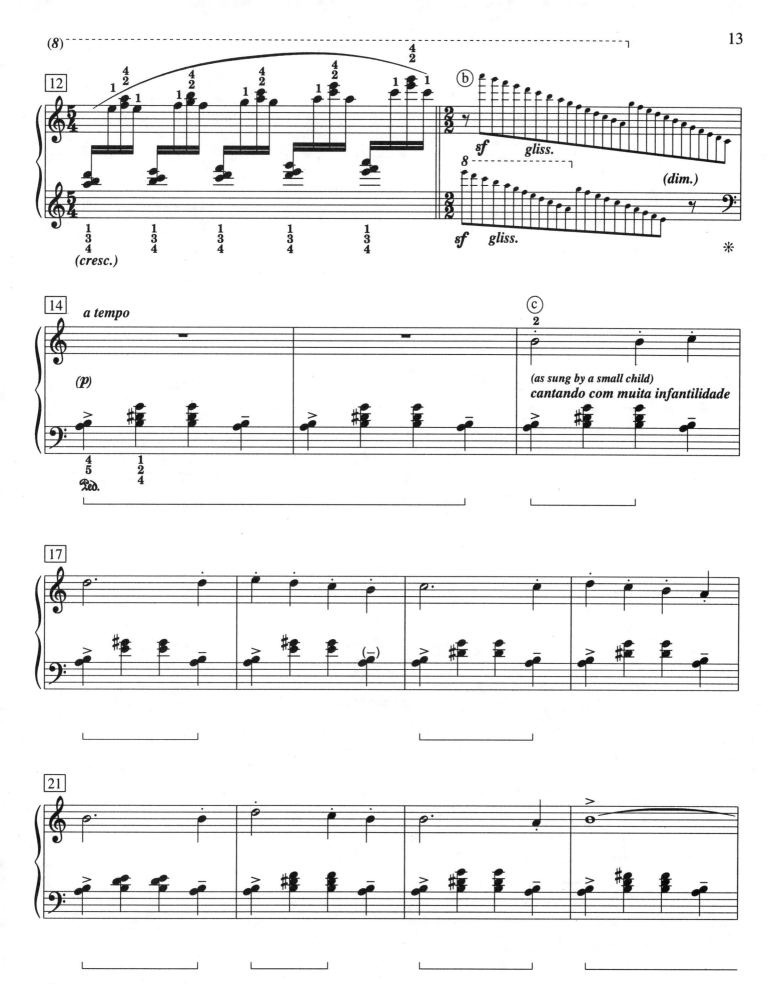

(b) The right-hand glissando should be played maintaining the thumbnail firmly against the keys while moving to the center of the keyboard. The left-hand glissando should be played with the fingernails of the second, third and fourth fingers firmly against the key. It is important that the fingers maintain a firm position to avoid injury to the hand.

(c) The melody in the right hand in measures 16–25 is a Brazilian folk lullaby, "Dorme, nenê."

14

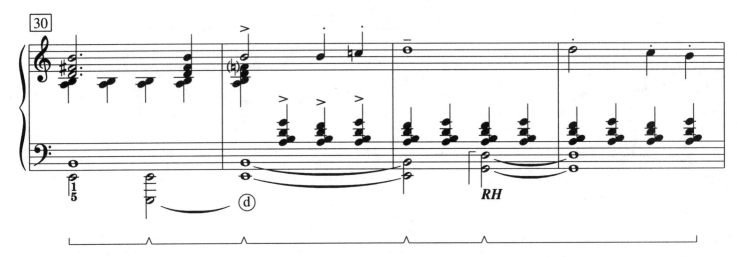

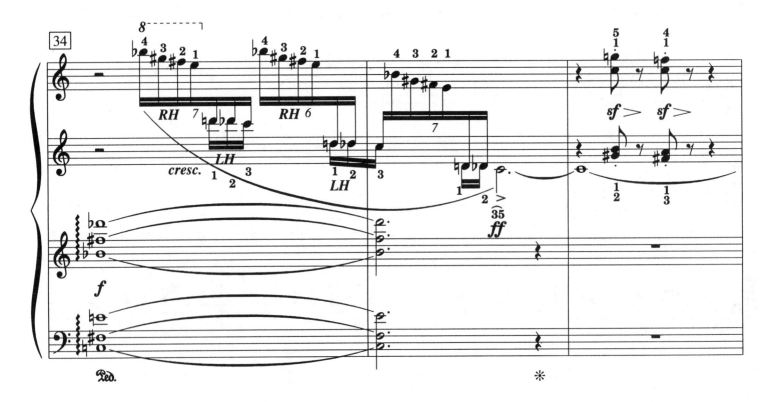

ⓓ The left-hand slur in measure 30 and the slurs in measures 40, 44 and 57 do not connect to other notes.
This is Villa-Lobos's indication, meaning to let the notes continue to sound beyond their indicated value.

ⓔ In measures 39–43 a variant of the "Dorme, nenê" melody appears in the second soprano voice in the right hand:

Because of Villa-Lobos's insistence that this melody be played clearly, in several editions the inner melody is notated separately from the chords.

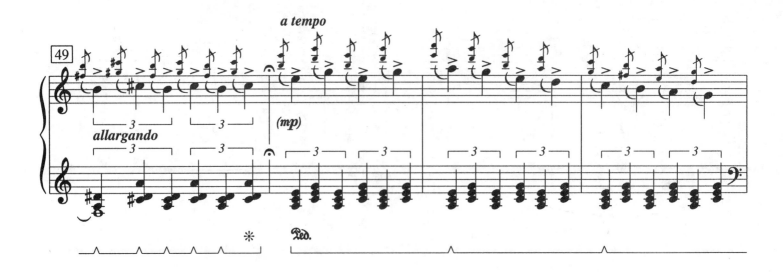

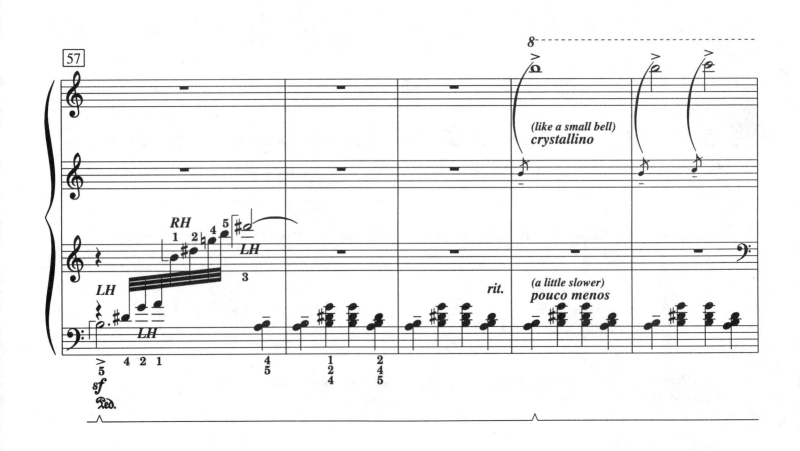

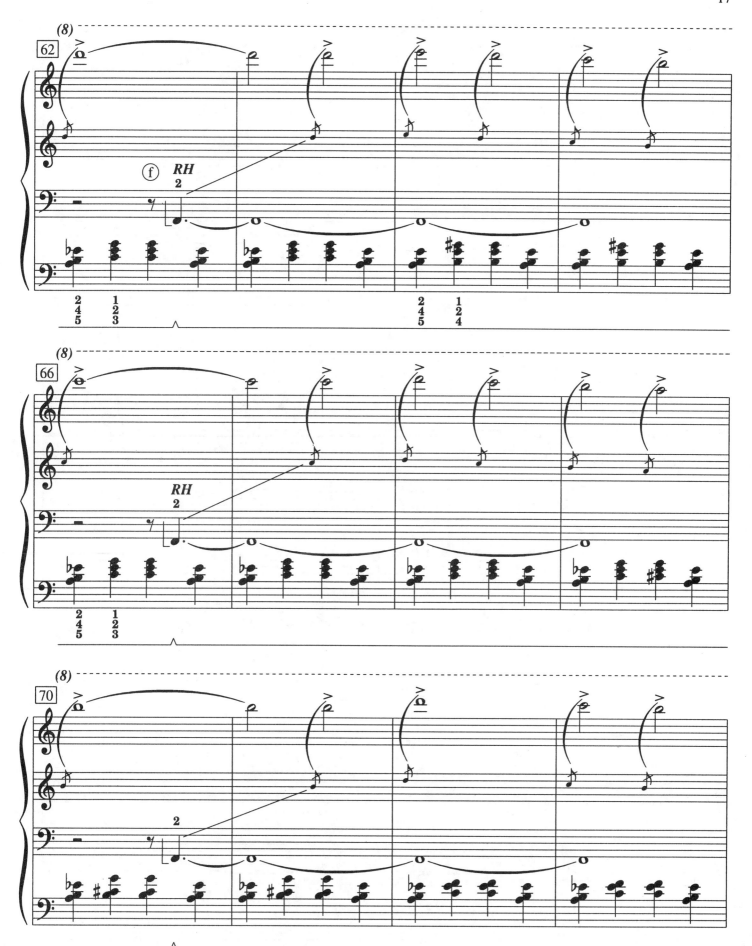

(f) The low F introduced at this point completes a three-part texture: the lullaby melody in the treble voice, a pattern of changing chords, and an ostinato low tone (F in measures 62, 66, 70 and 74, E in measures 79 and 82). The ideal sound is produced by maintaining the low notes with long damper pedals, keeping a clear, bell-like quality for the treble melody, and playing the chords pianissimo. This will produce a gentle blurring, suggesting a sleeping state of semiconsciousness. If technical difficulties make it difficult to play the chord changes pianissimo, more frequent pedal changes are suggested.

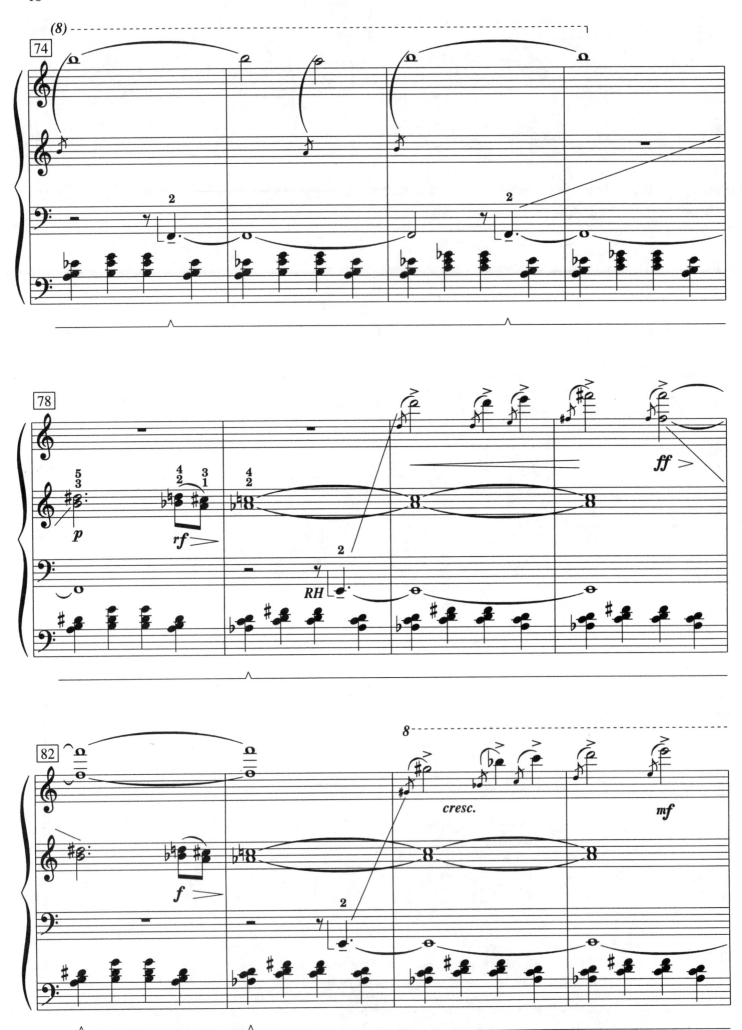

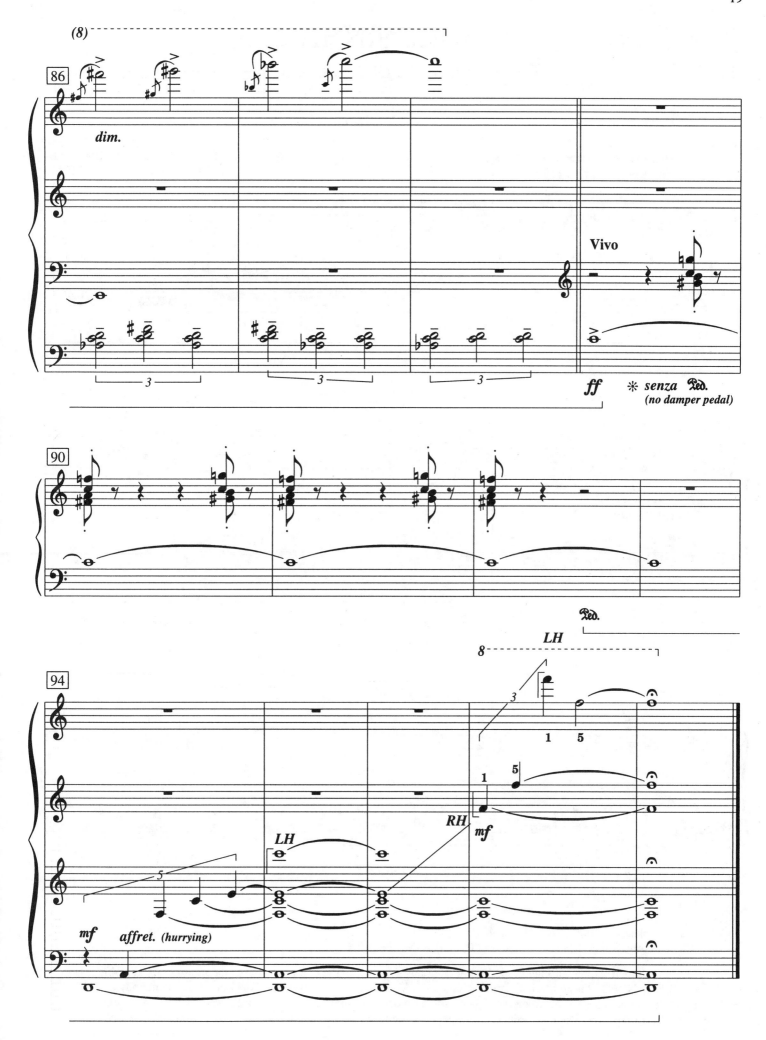

To Lucilia Villa-Lobos

MORENINHA

A BONECA DE MASSA ⓐ

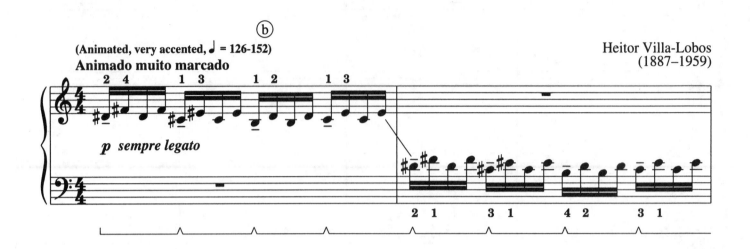

Heitor Villa-Lobos
(1887–1959)

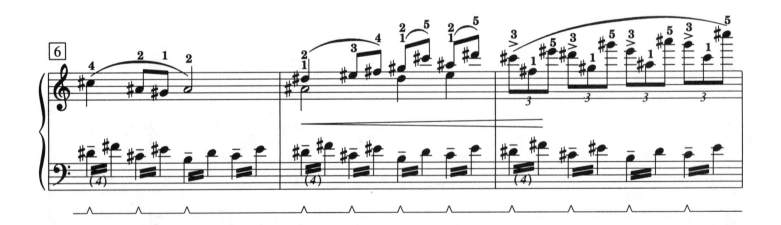

ⓐ Title and translation: *Moreninha* (The Little Brunette Doll)
Subtitle and translation: *A boneca de massa* (The Papier-Mâché Doll)

ⓑ The suggested metronome marking in the Eschig edition is ♩ = 144. In the editor's opinion, the minimum acceptable tempo is ♩ = 126, and ♩ = 152 is an ideal performance tempo. If Villa-Lobos's *mf* marking is maintained in the melody and the 16th-note patterns in the left hand (measure 3 and similar places) are played softly at ♩ = 152, pedal changes should be made each half measure. The four pedal changes per measure should be used at the slighty slower acceptable tempo.

ⓒ Chanté indicates that the melody in the left hand should be played with a songlike quality.

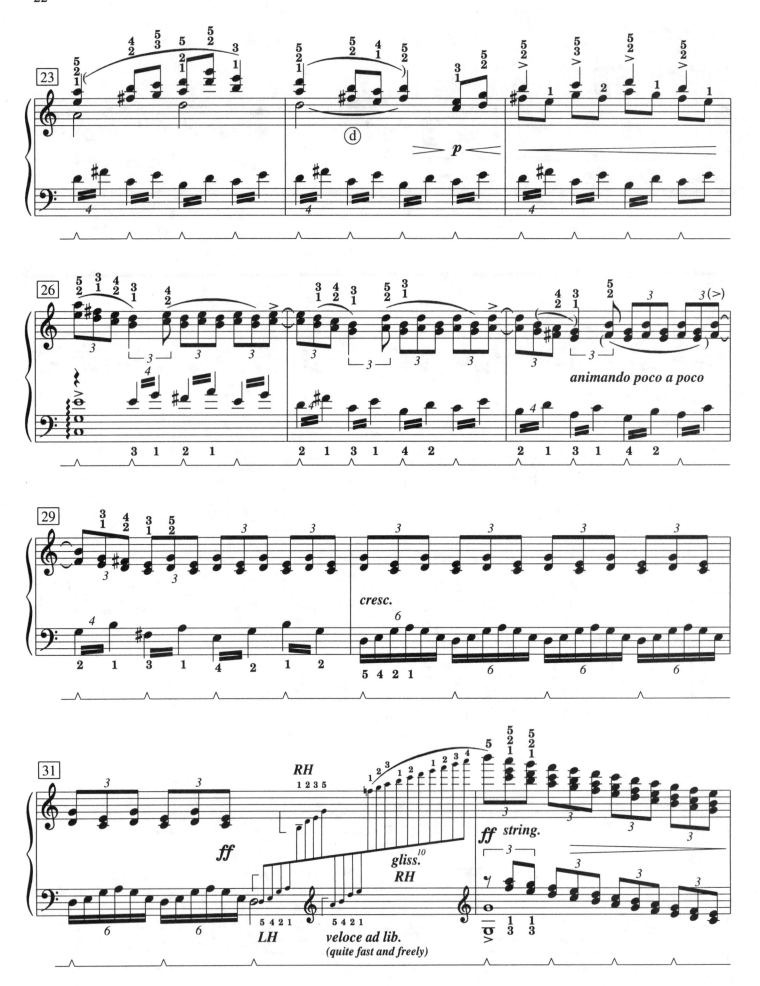

(d) The slur in measure 24 does not connect to other notes. This is Villa-Lobos's indication, meaning to let the note continue to sound beyond its indicated value.

To Lucilia Villa-Lobos

CABOCLINHA
A BONECA DE BARRO

Heitor Villa-Lobos
(1887–1959)

(a) Title and translation: *Caboclinha* (The Little Copper-Colored Doll)
Subtitle and translation: *A boneca de barro* (The Clay Doll)

(b) The rhythm pattern of 16th notes in groupings of 3+3+2 in duple meter is not only important in this piece, but is one of the most distinctive patterns in Brazilian music. The composer indicates a smooth sequence of connected 16th notes with a gentle undulating syncopation.

26

ⓒ The upper notes of the chords in the left hand in this section are a motive taken from the original melody and should be played so that the melodic significance is clear.

(A little faster)
Un peu animé

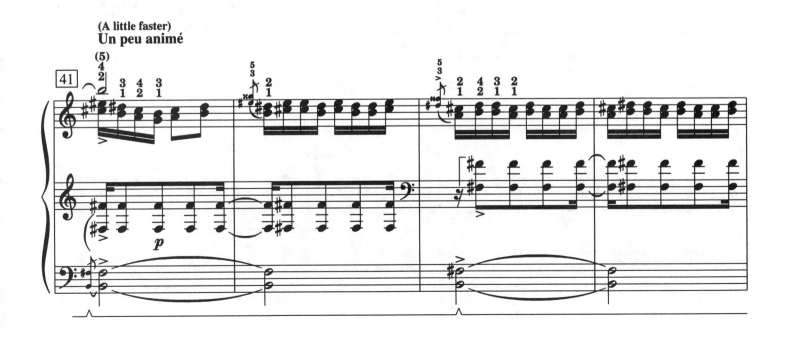

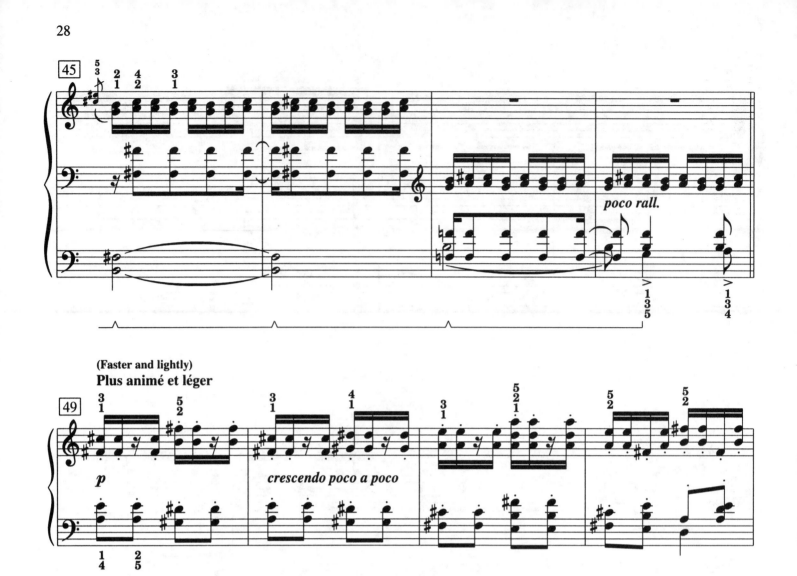

(Faster and lightly)
Plus animé et léger

(A tempo)
1er Mouvement

1er Mouvement

(d) The slurs in measure 74 do not connect to other notes. This is Villa-Lobos's indication, meaning to let the notes continue to sound beyond their indicated value.

To Lucilia Villa-Lobos

MULATINHA

A BONECA DE BORRACHA ⓐ

Heitor Villa-Lobos
(1887–1959)

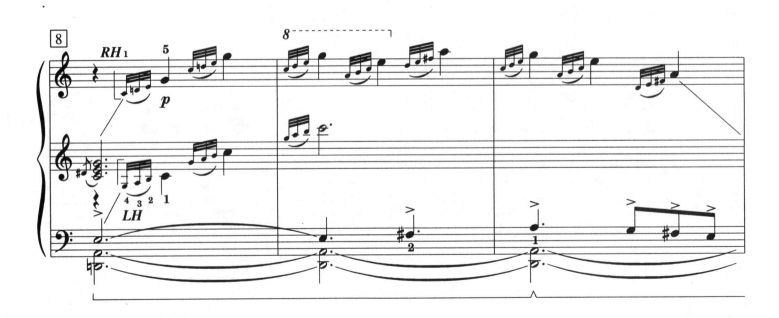

ⓐ Title and translation: *Mulatinha* (The Little Mulatto Doll)
Subtitle and translation: *A boneca de borracha* (The Rubber Doll)

(b) The accented notes, beginning with the final right-hand D in measure 12, are a rhythmic variant of the Brazilian folk melody "Vem cá, Bitú."

32

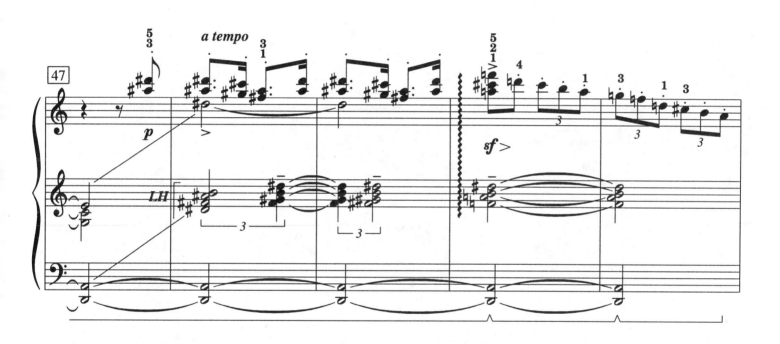

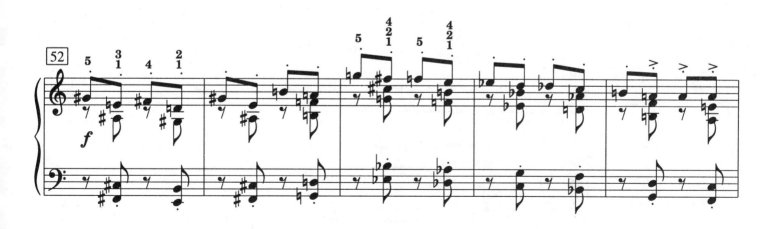

Ⓒ The slurs in measures 63, 70 and 74 do not connect to other notes. This is Villa-Lobos's indication, meaning to let the notes continue to sound beyond their indicated value.

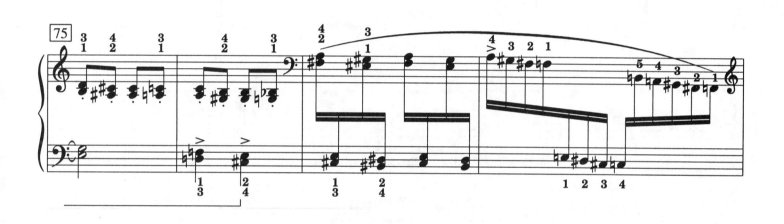

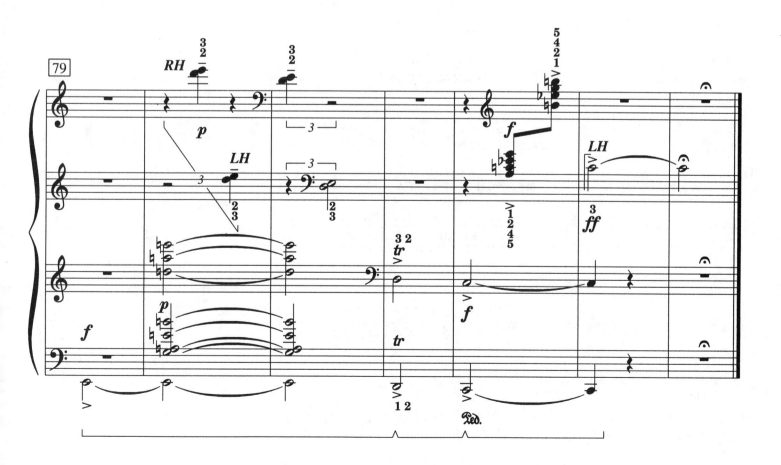

To Lucilia Villa-Lobos

NEGRINHA

A BONECA DE PAU ⓐ

Heitor Villa-Lobos
(1887–1959)

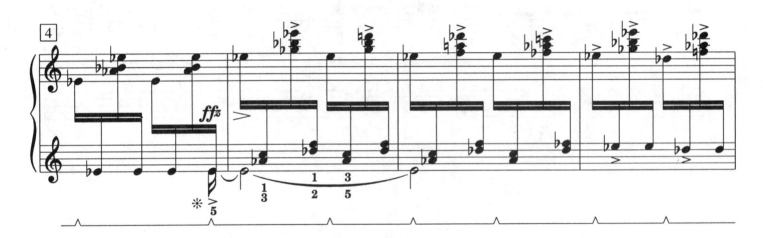

ⓐ Title and translation: *Negrinha* (The Little Black Doll)
   Subtitle and translation: *A boneca de pau* (The Wooden Doll)

ⓑ The slurs in measures 11, 15, 31, 35, 43, 47, 51, 57, 61 and 83 do not connect to other notes. This is Villa-Lobos's indication, meaning to let the notes continue to sound beyond their indicated value.

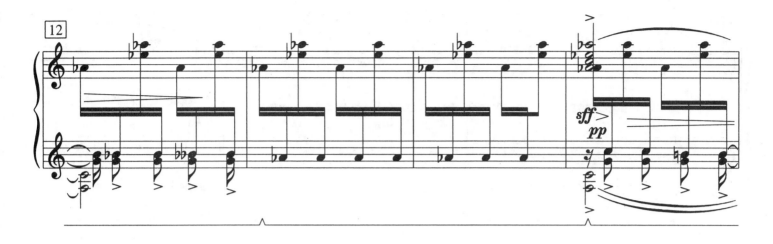

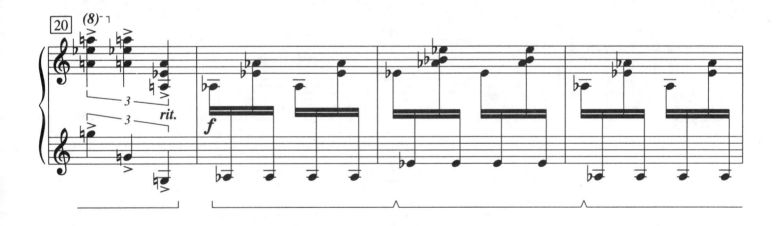

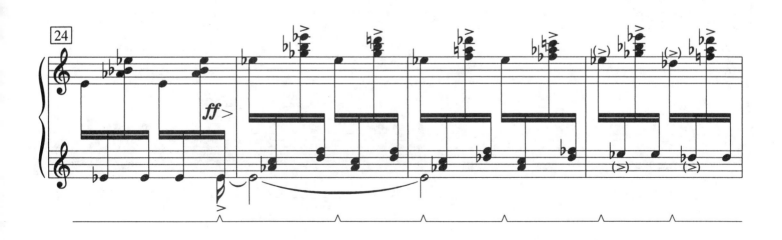

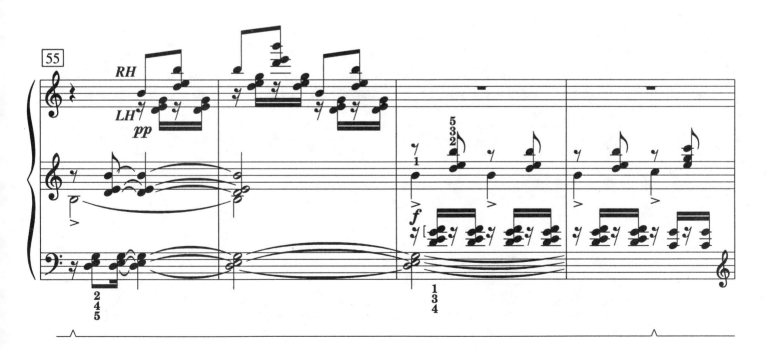

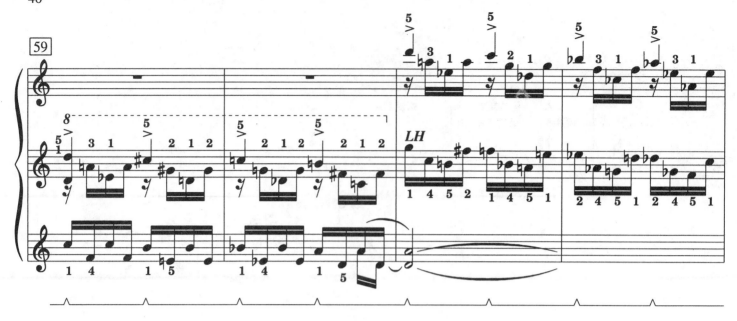

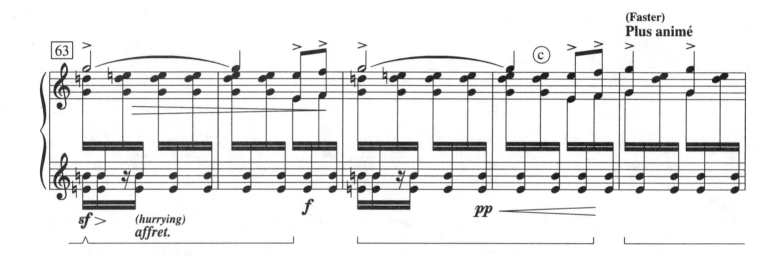

(c) The melody is a quotation from the *Guia prático* (No. 124, "Uma, duas angolinhas," translated as "One, Two Angolinhas").
The *angolinha* is a guinea hen, a pheasantlike bird. This folk song about a bird is one of the many quotations of Brazilian
melodies used by the composer.

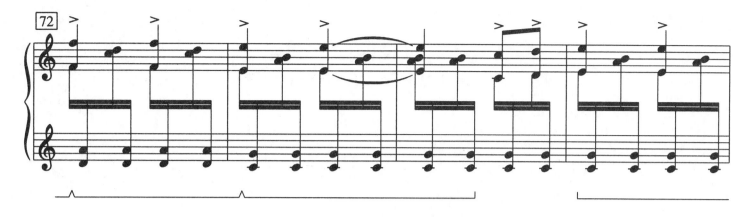

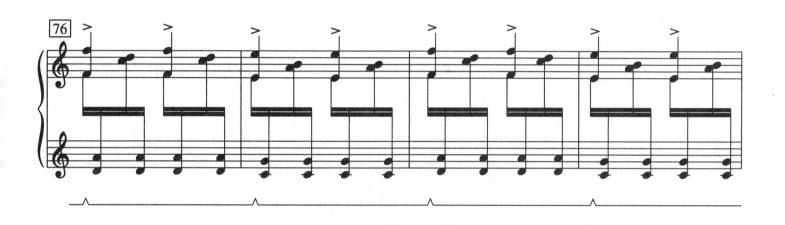

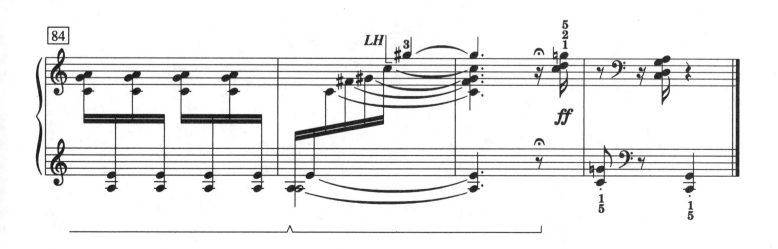

To Lucilia Villa-Lobos

A POBREZINHA
A BONECA DE TRAPO ⓐ

Heitor Villa-Lobos
(1887–1959)

(Slowly and with melancholy, ♩ = 42)
Lentamente e melancolico

ⓐ Title and translation: *A pobrezinha* (The Poor Little Doll)
Subtitle and translation: *A boneca de trapo* (The Rag Doll)

To Lucilia Villa-Lobos

O POLICHINELO

LE POLICHINEL

Heitor Villa-Lobos
(1887–1959)

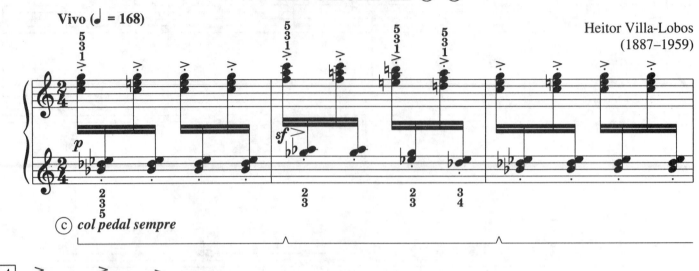

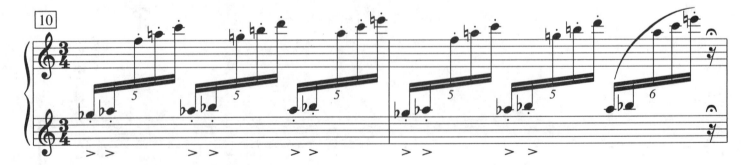

(a) Title and translation: *O polichinelo* (The Punch Doll)
Villa-Lobos does not use a subtitle, but repeats the title in French: *Le polichinel*

(b) When performing the complete set of eight movements, the order of the last two movements is frequently reversed, and the suite ends with "O polichinelo."

(c) The 1918 Napoleão edition has the marking "col pedal sempre" at the beginning of the piece. Pedaling will vary according to the performance tempo. When this movement is played at maximum tempo, very little pedal is necessary, and half pedals should be used.

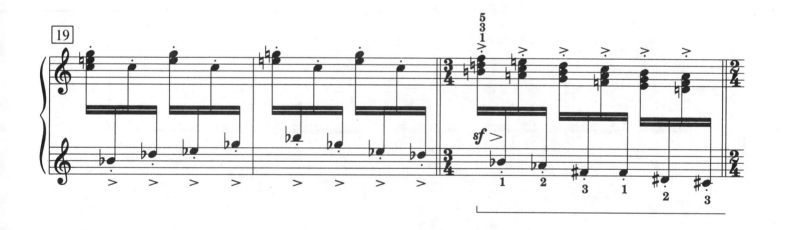

46

(d) The melody is a quotation of a well-known Brazilian folk tune, "Ciranda, Cirandinha" from the *Guia prático* (No. 35). *Ciranda* is a round dance, and *cirandinha* is a little round dance. The image conveyed is a group of children joyously singing a folk tune while dancing in a circle.

(e) The slur in measure 44 does not connect to another note. This is Villa-Lobos's indication, meaning to let the note continue to sound beyond its indicated value.

(f) Short accent pedals are recommended by the editor.

(g) The 1918 Napoleão edition ends with the fermata in measure 67. The glissando appears in a Museu Villa-Lobos copy of the 1918 Napoleão edition in the handwriting of the composer. Measure 68 appears for the first time in the Eschig edition.

(h) Even though the lowest bass note in this edition is written as C, an A is written as the bass note in all other known editions. The editor believes the final note should be a C octave, and this is confirmed on numerous recordings of the work.

To Lucilia Villa-Lobos

BRUXA
A BONECA DE PANO ⓐ

Heitor Villa-Lobos
(1887-1959)

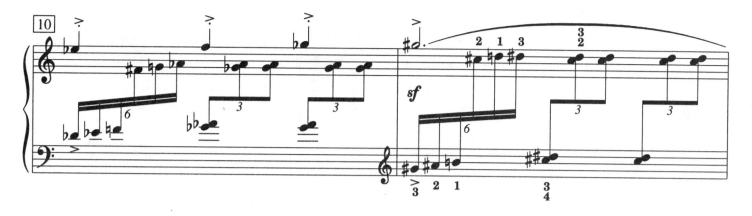

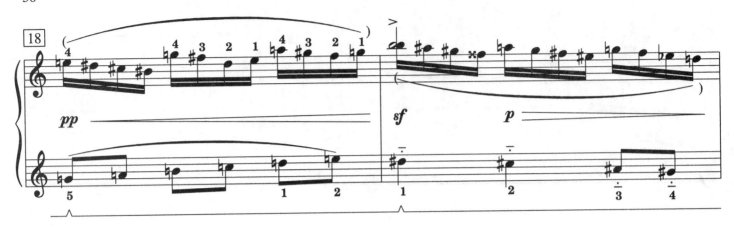

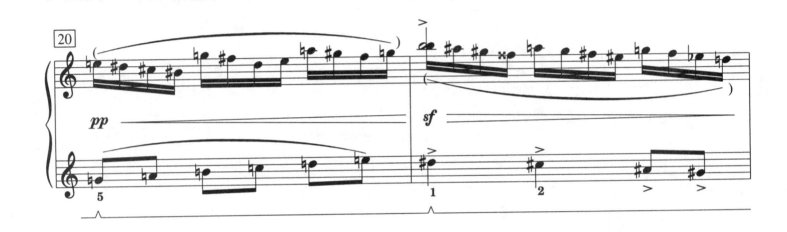

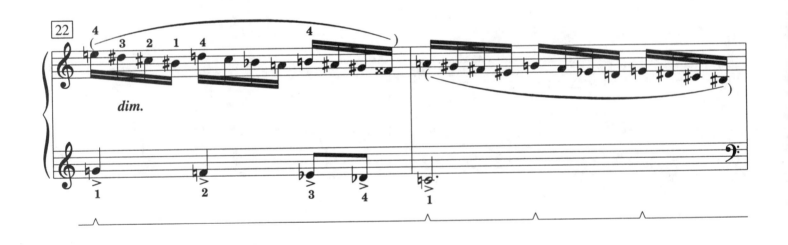

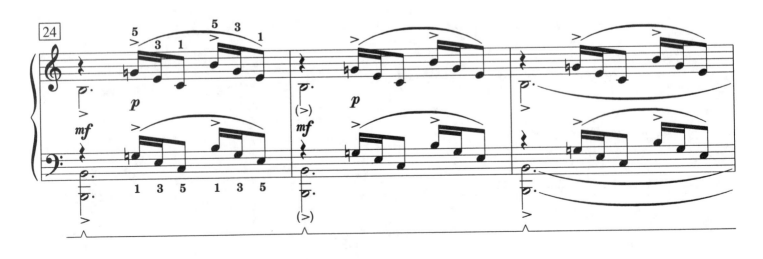

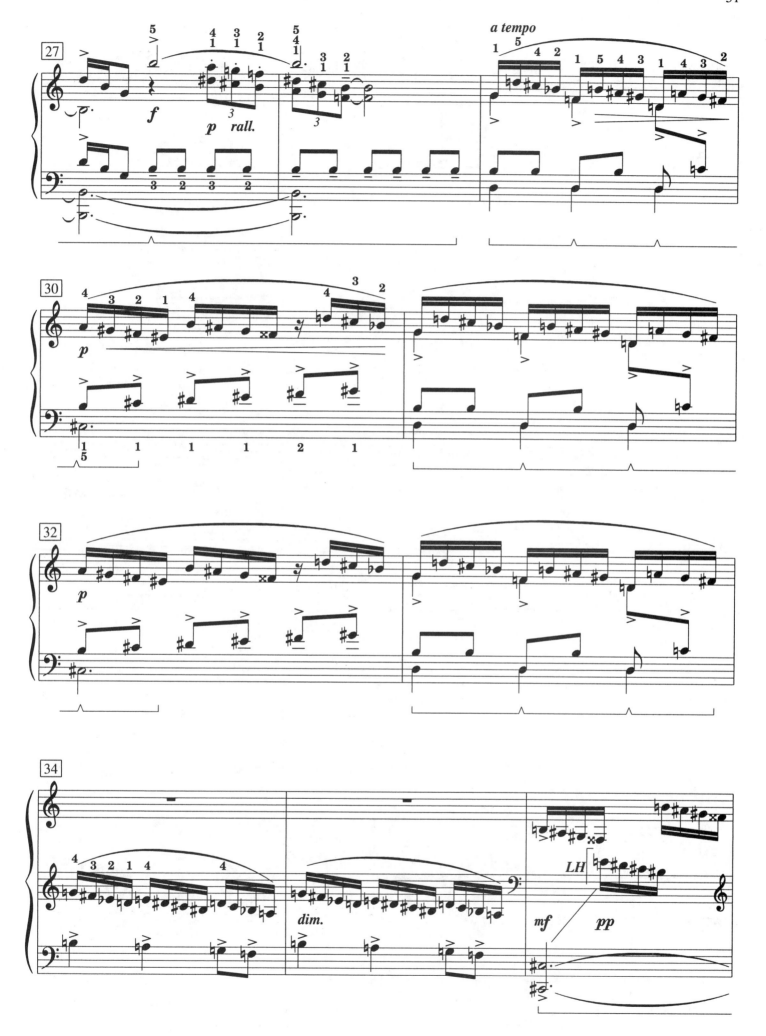

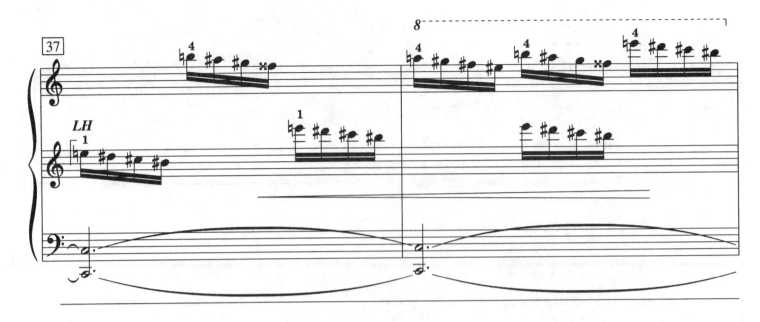

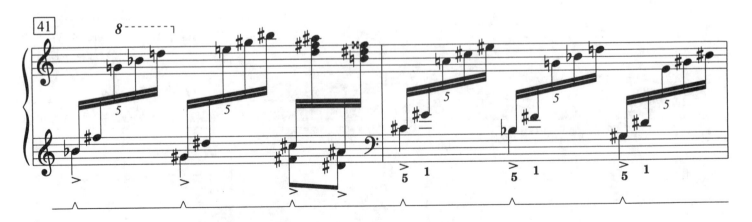

ⓑ The slurs in measures 39, 45, 47, 59, 61, 65, 67, 71, 73 and 88 do not connect to other notes.
This is Villa-Lobos's indication, meaning to let the notes continue to sound beyond their indicated value.

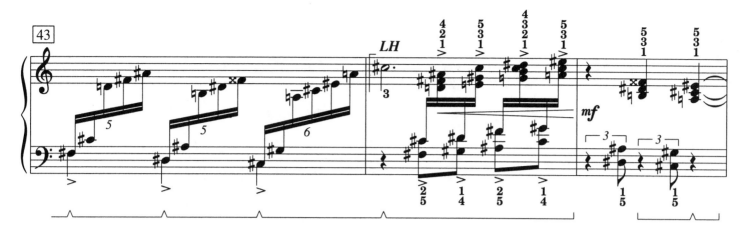

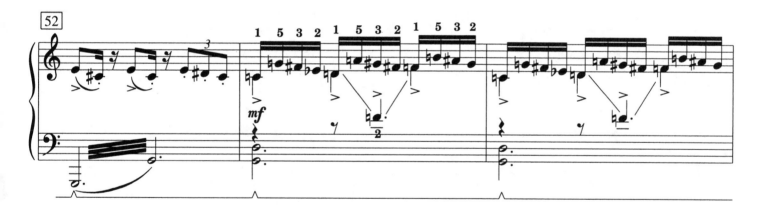

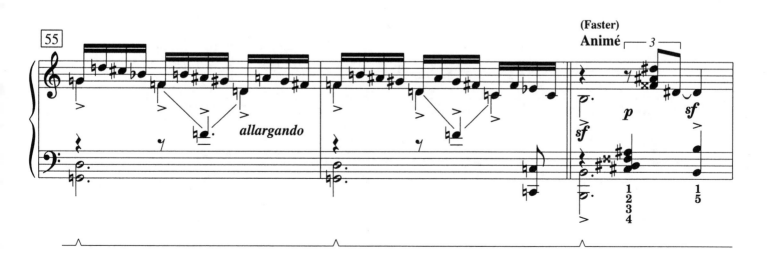

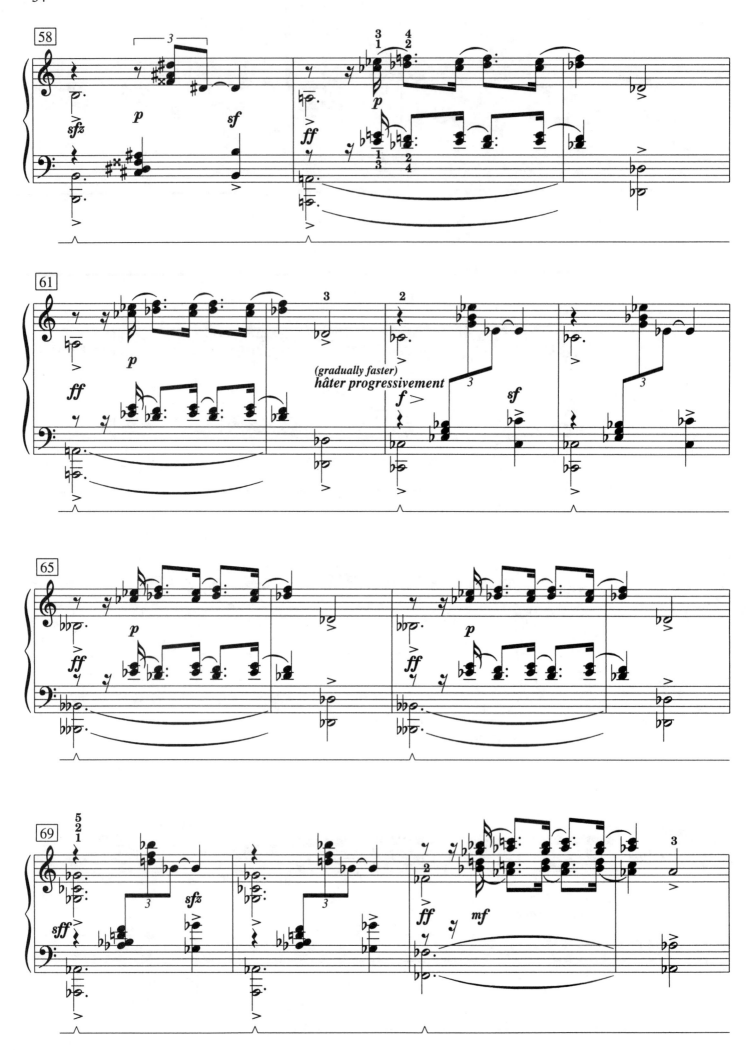

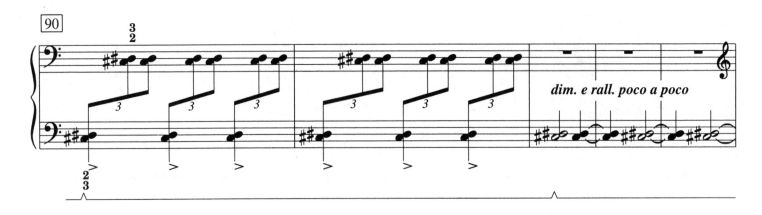

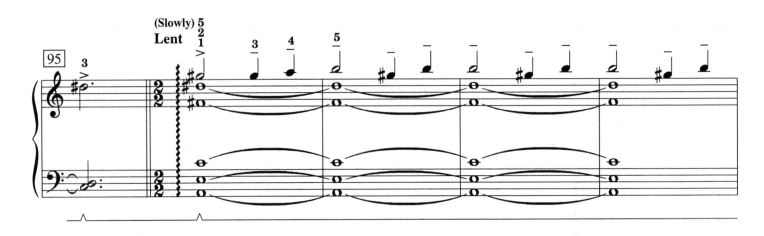

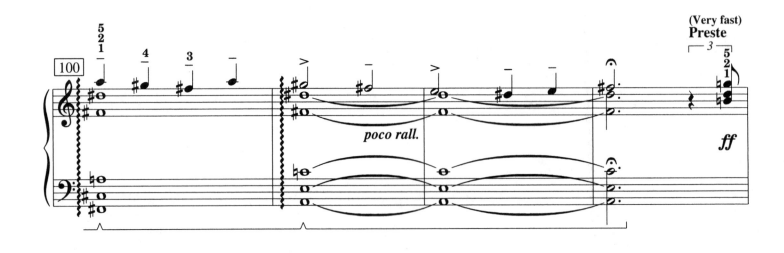